STUDENT TEACHERS' PERCEPTIONS OF THE PRE-SERVICE MATHEMATICS PROGRAMME IN A PRIMARY TEACHERS' COLLEGE IN ZIMBABWE

By

BARNABAS MUYENGWA

A DISSERTATION SUBMITTED TO THE FACULTY OF EDUCATION IN PARTIAL FULFILLMENT OF THE REQUIREMENTS FOR THE DEGREE OF MASTER OF EDUCATION IN TEACHER EDUCATION.

DEPARTMENT OF TEACHER EDUCATION
UNIVERSITY OF ZIMBABWE, HARARE

JUNE 1997

AuthorHouse™
1663 Liberty Drive
Bloomington, IN 47403
www.authorhouse.com
Phone: 1-800-839-8640

Published by AuthorHouse 12/17/2012

ISBN: 978-1-4772-5121-8 (sc)
ISBN: 978-1-4772-5122-5 (e)

UNIVERSITY OF ZIMBABWE

FACULTY OF EDUCATION

The undersigned certify that they have read and recommend to the University Senate for acceptance and approval a dissertation titled STUDENT TEACHERS' PERCEPTIONS OF THE PRE-SERVICE MATHEMATICS PROGRAMME IN A PRIMARY TEACHERS' COLLEGE IN ZIMBABWE submitted by *Barnabas Muyengwa* in partial fulfillment of the requirements for the Master of Education in Teacher Education degree.

....

Supervisor

....

External Examiner

....

Chairperson of the Department

....

Dean of the Faculty of Education
University of Zimbabwe, Harare
1997

UNIVERSITY OF ZIMBABWE

LIBRARY RELEASE FORM

NAME OF AUTHOR:	BARNABAS MUYENGWA
TITLE OF DISSERTATION:	Student Teachers' Perceptions Of The Pre-Service Mathematics Programme IN A Primary Teachers' College In Zimbabwe.
DEGREE FOR WHICH DISSERTATION	
WAS PRESENTED:	Master of Education
YEAR CONFERRED:	1997

Signature: ....

Address: 20 Gate Crescent
Zengeza 3
Chitungwiza

Date: 10 - 06 - 97

DEDICATION

This dissertation is dedicated to:

My Wife
Cordelia

My daughter
Rukudzo "Udzo"

and the
Muyengwa Family

ACKNOWLEDGEMENT

Acknowledgement is due and warmly extended to my supervisor Mr. C. Munetsi for the many valued discussions and helpful comments.

My special gratitude goes to colleagues at Seke Teachers' College for their well thought suggestions and the participating students for giving their time and trust.

Great thanks to Mrs. Muradzikwa who assisted me in capturing and analysing data and Mrs. Moyo who patiently typed this manuscript.

Last but not least, I wish to thank my wife, daughter, relatives and friends for their moral support.

TABLE OF CONTENTS

LIST OF TABLES

Abstract

This case study investigated the perceptions of the third year student teachers of the first year pre-service Mathematics programme at Seke Teachers' College in Zimbabwe. Student background characteristics of gender, age, teaching experience and Mathematics specialisation were the independent variables also investigated. Data was collected from 278 third year students enrolled for the general Diploma in Education course using questionnaires with a five point Likert type 33 item rating scale and open ended items. The data so collected were analysed both quantitatively and qualitatively.

The findings indicated that although the programme was able to provide students with a foundation in subject knowledge more could be done to improve on training in teaching methods and provision of resources. From the variables investigated gender was found to have an effect on students' perceptions of the programme but teaching experience was found to have no effect. The possible relationship between the independent variables of age and Mathematics specialisation and the dependent variable of students' perception of the programme was indicated in too few items to warrant a definite conclusion.

Implications for the improvement of the programme are that there is need for the college to revisit some aspects of the structure and organisation of the programme. There is also need for further research involving all primary teachers' colleges.

CHAPTER 1

INTRODUCTION

Programmes of initial teacher education are criticised for stressing theory and ideals at the expense of practice and reality. At present students in conventional primary teachers' colleges in Zimbabwe are trained for three years. The student teachers undergo training in both content and methods in the first year in preparation for teaching practice in the second year. In the final year students receive further training in both content and methods.

Although it is a truism that student teachers require pedagogical content knowledge to teach effectively, there is no agreement on what is sufficient and what is necessary pedagogical content knowledge (Meredith, 1993). There is need to evaluate pre-service programmes. The evaluation and improvement of instruction are closely linked because evaluation is seen as an instrument for enhancing the quality of teaching. An evaluation of a mathematics programme at a college based on students' perceptions can be used to improve the teaching strategies and classroom management skills of students (McCullogh and Mintz, 1992).

Research (Darley, Glucksberg, Kamin and Kinchla, 1982; De Cecco, 1968; and Luft 1969) underscores the importance of an individual having had an experience of something before they can formulate perceptions. Perceptions of a programme may be understood to imply an awareness of its existence. De Cecco (1968) indicates that our perceptions of events help in the formulation of appropriate concepts about that experience. While Darley et al (1981) view perceptions of an event as our educated guesses about the world we live in based on our prior experiences. Perceptions of an event or programme need not be uniform for any one group. McCullogh and Mintz (1992) observed that students who believe that their teacher training programme addresses significant questions about their future careers may have an easier transition into the classroom. Kasanda (1992) who evaluated the pre-service mathematics programme at the Copperbelt Secondary Teachers' College in Zambia noted that the programme was exposing trainee teachers to numerous strategies of teaching mathematics to a cross section of the Zambian secondary school population and equipping trainee teachers adequately for the hard task of teaching. In Zimbabwe, Nyikahadzoyi (1994) and Chihaka (1994) have called for great attention to be given to the form or mode of presentation of teacher preparation courses in Mathematics. It appears no study has been conducted in Zimbabwe which measures student teachers' perceptions of the pre-service Mathematics programme's ability to impart teaching strategies and classroom management skills to trainee teachers.

STATEMENT OF THE PROBLEM

The purpose of this study was to investigate the perceptions of the third year student teachers of the first year pre-service Mathematics programme at Seke Teachers' College in Zimbabwe.

Specifically, this study focuses on the subjects' perceptions of the programme's ability to impart both teaching strategies and classroom management skills to trainee teachers.

RESEARCH QUESTIONS

The study was to provide answers to the following questions:

1) Which of the student teachers' background characteristics had an effect on student teachers' perceptions of the pre-service Mathematics programme?

2) Which college inputs and teaching processes in preparation for teaching practice can improve the pre-service Mathematics programme?

VARIABLES

Among the independent variables investigated was student teachers' background characteristics such as the student teacher's gender, age, main subject specialisation of the student and the student's teaching experience prior to training.

The other independent variables investigated were the college inputs such as the staffing situation in the mathematics department, allocation of time for mathematics courses in the first year, resources, the teaching methods used, evaluation techniques and the content of the mathematics curriculum taught at college level. The college processes investigated were preparation for teaching practice.

The response variables consisted of the perceptions components: perceptions of the first year pre-service Mathematics programme's ability to impart teaching strategies and classroom management skills. It was not possible to investigate all the variables in the limited time that was available.

Research on student evaluations that includes teaching process variables is important mainly because it is crucial to establish just what it is specifically that students respond to when they make judgements about the worth of the teaching they experience (Dunkin, 1986). Dunkin (1986) argues that student evaluations are based partially on their perceptions of the teaching they receive. A number of factors influence perceptions. These include goals, attitudes, motives, past experiences, ability and also one's background and training (Wehmeier, 1991). Dubey (1986) believes that past experiences ensure perceptions of a given situation are made quickly. This implies that third year student teachers who have gone through the first two years of the pre-service Mathematics programme are likely to give accurate perceptions of the programme.

THE HYPOTHESES

The problem as stated shall be resolved with reference to the following hypotheses, stated here is the conventional null form:

1) Gender has no effect on student teachers' perceptions of the pre-service Mathematics programme.

2) Mathematics specialisation has no effect on student teachers' perceptions of the pre-service Mathematics programme.

3) Age has no effect on student teachers' perceptions of the pre-service Mathematics programme.

4) Teaching experience prior to training has no effect on student teachers' perceptions of the pre-service Mathematics programme.

PURPOSE OF THE STUDY

The purpose of this study is:

1) To find out whether the student teacher's gender has any effect on the student teacher's perception of the pre-service Mathematics programme.

2) The find out whether the student teacher's Mathematics specialisation in college has any effect on the student teacher's perception of the pre-service Mathematics programme.

3) To find out whether the age of a student has any effect on the student teacher's perception of the pre-service Mathematics programme.

4) To find out whether the student teacher's previous teaching experience prior to training has any effect on the student teacher's perception of the pre-service Mathematics programme.

5) To find out which college inputs and processes can improve the pre-service Mathematics programme.

ASSUMPTIONS OF THE STUDY

A number of assumptions were made for this study.

1) Perceptions of student teachers of the pre-service Mathematics programme are affected by the students' background characteristics.

2) The pre-service Mathematics programme is not imparting sufficient pedagogical knowledge and skills needed by students to effectively teach in the primary schools.

3) A gap exists between student preparation for teaching practice and student expectations for effective teaching practice.

4) Respondents will co-operate and provide truthful and valid information.

5) Perceptions can be readily measured.

6) Students' perceptions of the pre-service Mathematics programme can be used to appraise the programme.

THE SCOPE OF THE STUDY

This study focused on the independent variables of students' background characteristics, college inputs and processes and the dependent variables: perceptions: The study focused on third year students at Seke Teachers' College and the findings of this study are most likely to be peculiar to this college. The subjects of this study were third year students of 1997 who had gone through the first year pre-service Mathematics programme and had done their teaching practice in their second year.

LIMITATIONS OF THE STUDY

Within the limited time that was available for the study some variables, like teaching practice school characteristics and the student's performance on teaching practice, were not investigated. The researcher was a fulltime employee who was not sponsored in this study. Because of the time factor and costs the researcher could not draw data from all colleges in Zimbabwe. Financial constraints also forced the researcher to consider a smaller sample since a larger sample required more money for the production and processing of questionnaires.

SIGNIFICANCE OF THE STUDY

This study by investigating the perceptions of student teachers of the pre-service Mathematics programme can be used to update programmes in teachers' colleges to meet the needs of the students. It is hoped that through this research study the college will be able to evaluate its pre-service Mathematics programme and redesign it to meet the ever-changing needs of the student teachers on teaching practice.

This study will be of interest to lecturers, teachers, textbook publishers and curriculum planners in their endeavour to improve the standard of Mathematics education in teachers' colleges as well as in primary schools. It is also hoped that the findings of this study will provide useful empirical information for the improvement and development of primary teacher training programmes both at Seke Teachers' College and other primary teachers' colleges in Zimbabwe.

DEFINITION OF TERMS

Some important terms in this study have already been given treatment but for the purposes of clarity and in order to ensure that the terms would be used in the context to which they will be applied the researcher attempts further explanations of these terms.

Perception: In this study, perceiptions can be referred to as a point view which is a result of a particular way of understanding a situation, event or message.

Student teacher: A student teacher is a person, usually above the age of eighteen and either male or female, studying at a College of Education for the purpose of acquiring a teaching qualification and hoping to take up teaching as a profession.

Pre-service Mathematics programme: In this study pre-service Mathematics programme refers to all Mathematics courses on content and/or methodology studied by student teachers.

Classroom management skill: Classroom management skill is the acquired ability or proficiency in the art of carefully preparing, presenting, disciplining and controlling class activities.

Teaching strategy: A teaching strategy is a way or plan of carrying out instructional and managerial activities. Instructional activities are intended to facilitate the pupils' achievement of specific educational objectives. Managerial activities, on the other hand, are intended to create and maintain condition sin which instruction can take place effectively.

Teaching practice: Alternative terms for teaching practice are student teaching, field experience, practice teaching, practicum and school experience.

Evaluation: Evaluation is the process of determining the worth of a thing. Evaluation deals with the appraisal of value or worth of a thing, process or programme.

Main subject: A main subject is a student teacher's subject of specialisation. Each student teacher has one subject in which he/she studies to advance his/her academic content knowledge in that subject to a level beyond Ordinary Level and at times slightly beyond Advanced Level.

Professional Studies: In Professional Studies student teachers are exposed to a multiplicity of curriculum courses which act as an introduction to the basic content of a range of subjects in the primary school, as well as insight into how to teach them.

Applied Mathematics: Applied Mathematics refers to Professional Studies Mathematics Syllabus B which focuses on how to teach Mathematics in the primary school.

CHAPTER 2

LITERATURE REVIEW

INTRODUCTION:

Criticisms that teacher education is too theoretical have appeared in a study flow in recent years, both in the United Kingdom and in much of the rest of the English speaking world (Griffiths and Tann, 1992). The present writer is of the opinion that teacher education is attacked because it is over-full of theory in contrast with down-to-earth practice. Conventional teacher education programmes follow an apprenticeship model and in so doing aspire to provide student teachers with pedagogical skills and techniques (Zeichner and Liston, 1988). McNamara (1990), together with other recent contributors to the debate on how best to educate teachers (for example Solomon, 1987; Stones, 1989), agrees on the centrality of pedagogy.

A serious concern of teacher education is the absence of a universally accepted body of practitioner knowledge. Teacher education programmes are not systematically teaching that knowledge to new practitioners. A recognised knowledge base and a repertoire of behaviours and skills are essential for teacher education programmes to adequately prepare students for teaching. Watts (1982) observed that "these programmes appear to be teaching best what the practitioners need least, and teaching least what the practitioners need most" (p. 39).

Both teacher educators and student teachers share similar aims and concerns about developing professional competence, and although teacher educators design courses to this end, students do not always perceive this to be the case. The instruction experienced by the students may be different from the intended instruction; or the instruction may not be understood or perceived by the students. Wittrock (1986) found that the student's perception of teaching influences student learning and achievement.

Despite the enormous emphasis currently being placed on the improvement of development of teacher education programmes in Zimbabwe, the number of studies devoted to the evaluation of these programmes to determine to what extent they are achieving their objectives seem to be surprisingly meagre. Previous review of the programmes (Shumba, 1991; Chivore, 1991) have been influenced largely by impressions of the programme staff about the way the programme is being operated and also comments by external assessors. The students seem to have contributed little in the review of the programmes. The present study seeks, as one of its aims, to use students' perceptions to evaluate the first year pre-service Mathematics programme. Choppin (1977), however warned of the danger of the 'Hawthorne effect' when using students' perceptions in evaluating a programme.

Students' Perceptions of a Programme

Students' perceptions can be used to evaluate a teaching programme. Perceptions of a programme are likely to be influenced by motives, attitudes, past experience, emotional state, ability and one's background (Louw and Edwards, 1993). In the words of Dunkin and Barnes (1986: 769):

> Psychological research over many decades has demonstrated clearly that personal attributes and general features of the environment do influence perceptions and judgements and there is no reason to expect students are immune to these influences in their perceptions and evaluations of teaching.

Thus in this study student teachers' background characteristics such as gender, age, teaching experience and subject specialisation are among the independent variables being investigated. There is the matter of the effects of extraneous variables upon student perceptions. Commonly expressed views are that students are biased by extraneous factors such as the sex, popularity of the tutor, and students are more negative toward more demanding courses (Dunkin and Barnes, 1986). The present writer has, through experience, noted that Mathematics courses are considered difficult by most student teachers. This implies that most students could be having a negative attitude towards Mathematics programmes.

Dunkin and Bernes (1986) seem to have made two important observations. First, reviewers of the literature on student perceptions (Costin, Greenough and Menges, 1971; McKeachie, 1979; Menges 1979) concluded that student evaluations were not unduly affected by extraneous elements. Second, it seems from research students are able to perceive variations in teaching processes, and that the latter, more than extraneous elements, affect student perceptions of teaching.

Akpe (1988) carried out a study aimed at evaluating a Nigerian college of education programme using students' perceptions of the programme. He found that female students seemed more satisfied with the programme than their male counterparts. His second observation was that students who had prior teaching experience seemed more satisfied than those who had never been teachers.

These findings had a strong bearing on this study which sought to investigate the effect of a student teacher's gender and teaching experience on the student teacher's perception of the first year pre-service Mathematics programme's ability to impart both teaching strategies and classroom management skills to trainee teachers.

Inputs and Processes

College inputs and processes are some of the major factors in the production process for teacher education. Inputs are the resources used in the production activity and Windham (1988) observes that inputs may be divided into the general categories of student characteristics, college characteristics, tutor characteristics, instructional material and equipment characteristics, and facilities characteristics. In this case the term "characteristics" refers to the availability of a resource, its nature and quality, and its manner and rate of utilisation.

The process stage of educational production refers to the means by which educational inputs are transformed into educational outputs. Outputs are the direct and immediate effects of the educational process. They include such things as attitudinal changes, behavioural changes, cognitive achievement and manual skill development (Windham, 1988)

In the process stage teachers' colleges must prepare student teachers to teach effectively and efficiently. This implies a pre-service Mathematics programme must aim to extend and deepen a student's understanding of mathematics in order to provide students with specialist knowledge of teaching mathematics.

As part of the process stage student teachers are taught subject content, teaching methods and classroom management skills. The focus of this study is to determine whether student teachers are adequately prepared in subject content, pedagogical content knowledge and classroom management skills in the first year pre-service Mathematics programme. One of the basic research questions of this study focuses on the college inputs and teaching processes in preparation for teaching practice which can improve the pre-service Mathematics programme.

College Inputs

Staffing

McCullogh and Mintz (1992; 59) recommended that:

> Teacher educators need to be aware of the knowledge base of teaching, theories of teacher development, and how best to teach student teachers so that they are prepared for teaching.

From the above statement, it would appear college lecturers have to be highly qualified and experienced. The implications are that the task of training effective teachers requires two kinds of empirical knowledge: knowledge about how training contributes to the acquisition of teaching skills and knowledge about how teaching skills influence pupil learning.

Content of Course

Watts (1982) observed that the professional studies component of teacher education programmes should be designed to teach appropriate pedagogical knowledge, skills, and abilities needed in successfully practising the teaching profession. Pedagogical knowledge forms the essential bridge between academic subject matter knowledge and the teaching of subject matter. Transformation is at the heart of pedagogical knowledge since 'comprehended ideas must be transformed in some way if they are to be taught' (Shulman 1987, p. 16). Because of its largely practical origins, pedagogical knowledge of teaching subject matter has been termed practical knowledge (Elbaz, 1983) as it includes the practical skills of transforming subject matter for teaching and skills for teaching it (Ernest, 1989).

Student teachers begin to acquire their knowledge of mathematics teaching during their student years, on the basis of their learning experiences (Ernest, 1989). They learn mathematics pedagogy during their pre-service teacher education in methodology courses. Classroom management skills are also taught in these courses. Classroom management includes the organisation of certain non-academic tasks which are essential for effective teaching (Brown and Brown, 1992). It consists of checking class attendance, keeping a record of class progress, controlling pupils' conduct and activities, manipulating instructional materials, the improvement of classroom working conditions and the elimination of any distractions which may arise. The present study wishes to find out whether the first year pre-service Mathematics programme was able to impart teaching strategies and classroom management skills to trainee teachers.

Some studies have been conducted to investigate the relationship between practitioner needs and competencies developed at colleges of education. Pigge (1978) in Watts (1982) found a -0.20 negative correlation between ranks of practitioner needs and competencies developed at a college of education. Yarger, Howey, and Joice (1977) in Watts (1982) discovered that twenty percent of the programmes they investigated provided no training in classroom organisation and management, while thirty-five percent lacked training in the diagnosis and remediation of learning difficulties. In Zambia, Kasanda (1992) concluded from the findings of his study of 227 former students of the Copperbelt Secondary Teachers' College that students perceive the Mathematics programme as able to impart teaching strategies and classroom management skills.

Whilst the findings of these studies seem to contradict each other, they raise issues which have a bearing on this research study. The development of the curriculum for teacher education courses should address the practitioners' needs for them to teach effectively in the schools. The present study wishes to answer the question: Is the first year pre-service Mathematics programme transmitting the pedagogical knowledge, skills and abilities necessary to effectively perform the duties of a teacher?

Resources

The pedagogical methods utilised in teachers' colleges could make use of the most up-to-date and effective resources and technology. That, apparently, is not the case. Yarger and Joyce (1977) in Watts (1982) reported that colleges of education do not take advantage of technology in their teacher preparation courses. They observed that the use of videotaping, microteaching, simulation and interaction analysis is not typical of these courses. The situation seems to be worse in developing countries.

The World Bank (1988) reports that the shortage of teaching and learning materials in the classroom is probably the most important obstacle in the way of effective teacher education. The present writer is of the opinion that it is the unavailability of resources that shows the greatest gap between this continent and the rest of the world. This implies that teacher education programmes need new ideas to be more responsive to the call of the use of appropriate technology.

College processes

Preparation for Teaching Practice

Preparation for teaching practice is one of the processes in teacher education programmes. Teaching practice is an important component of teacher education programmes world wide. Cohen and Manion (1977) see teaching practice as initiation of the student teacher into the teaching profession or the total experience of schools acquired by students during their periods of attachment. It involves practising of various teaching skills associated with the role of the teacher. This means that teaching practice enables a student teacher to put theory learned at college into practice. Among the skills and attributes to be developed during teaching practice are lesson preparation, planning, presentation, classroom management and documentation.

College based pre-service teacher education programmes are accountable for transmitting the knowledge, skills and abilities necessary for the successful practice of teaching in the schools. Proctor (1984) asserts that the professional skills which initial training give to an intending teacher lie at the heart of the training process. The methodology courses in teachers' colleges could be used to impart professional skills to trainee teachers. This study wishes to find out, using student teachers' perceptions, whether students are adequately prepared for teaching practice.

Brown and Brown (1992) argue that if the student teachers are well prepared in the following four areas:—theoretical knowledge about learning and human behaviour, attitudes that reinforce learning and human relationships; knowledge of the subject matter to be taught; and control of technical skills of teaching that facilitate pupil learning;—they should encounter very few problems in achieving success in teaching. The present writer thinks that initial teacher education programmes could address all the mentioned four areas to fully prepare students for teaching practice.

Micro-teaching

Micro-teaching is one of the very useful ways of training teachers in important instructional skills. The method was devised by Dwight Allen with a team of teachers and researchers at Stamford University, California (Farrant, 1981). Micro-teaching is a scaled down teaching encounter that has been developed as a preliminary experience and practice in teaching. In micro-teaching the student teacher has the opportunity to plan and practice a wide array of new instructional strategies.

The present writer thinks that the ability to focus on a particular aspect of lesson teaching is one of the major advantages of using micro-teaching. For example, in a session one could focus on the introduction, lesson development or closure. This reduction of the lesson into smaller parts is likely to enhance skill development.

Farrant (1981) concedes that some of the advantages of micro-teaching are that it enables separate skills to be practised and perfected without the distractions of classroom management and provides opportunity for immediate feedback and repetition.

Critics of micro-teaching have argued that the setting is 'artificial' and is not sufficiently comparable to the classroom for the transfer of skill development. The other disadvantage of videotaped micro-teaching is that the presence of a recording machine may serve as a deterrent in effective teaching. As the student is conscious that mistakes will be recorded he/ she will make more mistakes in an attempt to avoid them.

Despite some of these criticisms, micro-teaching could be seriously considered as a teaching method as it is better than presenting the student teacher in a 'sink-or-swim' environment in which he/she has to attend to every instructional consideration. It would appear most teachers' colleges in this country lack up-to-date equipment for video taped micro-teaching and the large number of students in methodology classes could also be another limiting factor.

In a study carried out with student teachers Pauline (1993) found micro-teaching to be an efficient way to have students in methods classes plan, teach and evaluate a lesson presented to a small class. This study wishes to find out if micro-teaching was used to impart teaching strategies to trainee teachers.

Subject matter knowledge

Knowledge of subject matter provides a foundation for the teacher's pedagogical knowledge and sills for teaching the subject. Thus a good command of the subject matter to be taught is very necessary for the teacher's success in the classroom. Shulman (1986) terms the role of subject matter knowledge in teaching the 'missing program' in research on teacher cognitions, and argues that knowledge of teaching will not advance until this lack is addressed. This could mean that the different types of knowledge of the teacher and their relationship with practice have to be understood.

It seems the centrality of subject matter knowledge in Mathematics programmes in teacher education cannot be disputed. Ernest (1989: 16) has this to say on the importance of mathematical knowledge:

> Whatever means of instruction are adopted the teacher needs a substantial knowledge base in the subject in order to plan for instruction and to understand and guide the learner's responses.

This could mean that the teacher's knowledge of mathematics is central to the planning of instruction and in the teaching process as it underpins the teacher's explanations, demonstrations, diagnosis of children's own methods and curriculum decisions.

The need for subject matter mastery by teachers is supported by Fennema, Carpenter and Peterson (1992) who argue that teachers must have in-depth knowledge not only of the specific mathematics they teach, but also of the mathematics that their students are to learn in future. Igboko (1976) also argues for a deeper and wider content knowledge of mathematics by alleging that this makes the teacher have the necessary competence for facing his or her class with confidence.

A number of studies have been carried out on the relationship between knowledge of mathematics content and teaching the subject. Brown, Cooney and Jones (1992) carried out a review of studies about elementary pre-service teachers' knowledge of content. They concluded that the studies gave the impression that pre-service elementary teachers do not posses a level of mathematical understanding that is necessary to teach elementary school mathematics as recommended in various proclamations from professional organisations.

In a study carried out by Fennema et al (1992) the conclusion was that instruction and subsequent learning were richer in the area in which the teacher was more knowledgeable than in areas where the teacher had less knowledge. In a different study Grossman, Wilson and Shulman (1989) found out that teachers' subject matter knowledge has an effect on what they teach, as well as on how they teach it.

The findings of these studies seem to suggest that subject matter knowledge is important. This study seeks to find out student teachers' views on the adequacy of the subject matter knowledge they were given in college in preparation for teaching practice.

Professional Training

Teaching skills can be taught, and, when they are not, student teachers rely on whatever they have learned through personal experience. Many student teachers embark on their training with very firmly fixed ideas of teachers and teaching especially if they have decided to be teachers by their early secondary school years (Carpenter, 1981). This could imply that all practice is an expression of personal theory. Writers such as Carr and Kemmis (1986), Schon (1983) and Elliot (1989) argue that all action is an expression of theory.

Some deficiencies related to the professional preparation of teachers in the areas of planning, evaluating learning and classroom management skills have been observed in some studies on teacher education programmes. Morrison and McIntyre (1969) found that student teachers had problems of how to plan and evaluate their lessons so as to improve their performance.

Morris and Stones (1972) suggested that student teacher shortcomings included planning and preparation of lessons, evaluation of learner progress and the acquisition of appropriate skills.

An overview of the findings of external assessors on teaching practice carried out by Shumba (1991), revealed that although the majority of student teachers made an effort to maintain their schemes and lesson plans up to date, there were major shortfalls in the plans including: objectives being non-behavioural, lack of or inadequate introduction and/or closure, problems of sequencing, lack of reference to teaching aids, poor evaluations, and failure to make provision for slow learners. He pointed out that 'these were all weaknesses which the colleges can remedy during pre-service training' (p. 9). Professional training given to student teachers whilst in college was investigated in this present study.

Summary

This chapter discussed and reviewed available and related literature on selected variables that are likely to affect student teachers' perceptions of a teaching programme. This study seeks to extend the findings to student teachers at Seke Teachers' College to assess their perceptions of the first year Mathematics programme's ability to impart teaching strategies and classroom management skills to trainee teachers. The next chapter gives an account of the research design and the data collection methodology for this study.

CHAPTER 3

METHODOLOGY

This chapter presents the research design for the study, data collection procedures and data analysis.

Research Design

The research design was a case study of Seke Teachers' College. Considering the time available, the nature of the research questions and the subjects available for the study, the researcher decided to adopt the case study research design. Teachers' colleges are unique in the sense that each college designs its own syllabus which is used by the lecturing staff and also the quantity and quality of material and equipment vary from college to college.

This case study focused on gaining deeper insight into student teachers' perceptions of the first year pre-service Mathematics programme's ability to impart teaching strategies and classroom management skills to trainee teachers. Isaac and Michael (1984) observe that, while the case study is weak on ideas of sampling and control, it has the ability to give deep insight into issues in this case, student teachers' perceptions of the first year pre-service Mathematics programme.

Participants

Participants were third year pre-service student teachers enrolled in the general course of the Diploma in Education (DE) at Seke Teachers' College in 1997. While all students in this course were invited to participate in this study, there was a 93.6% response rate from the concerned students. A total of 278 students participated in this study with ages ranging from 20 years to 35 years. There were 110 females and 168 males.

The third year students were used in this study because they had gone through the first year pre-service Mathematics programme and had done their teaching practice during their second year of training in 1996. These students were considered to be competent enough to respond to questions on the first year pre-service Mathematics programme.

Research Instruments

To collect data it was necessary to develop an instrument which would assist the researcher to get the information on the students' perceptions of the first year pre-service Mathematics programme. A student teachers' perceptions questionnaire with three sections was developed (see Appendix I). The first section asked for personal information—sex and age of the respondent, subject specialisation and teaching experience prior to joining college. The second section was a thirty-three item five point Likert type scale, the first year pre-service Mathematics programme rating scale to which all respondents were required to indicate the intensity of their agreement or disagreement with each of the statements on the scale as applied to the first year pre-service Mathematics programme. The third section was on student observations of the first year pre-service Mathematics programme and suggestions on how it could be improved.

Items on teaching method and classroom management skills were adapted from Kasanda (1992) and Chawanji (1992). These were adapted to suit the requirements of this case study. The questionnaire used to collect data was carefully designed to prevent the respondents from guessing what was being investigated in order to avoid influenced responses. To perfect the questionnaire, lecturers at Seke Teachers' College were asked to read and correct the questionnaire items. After corrections, the instrument was then administered to a group of second year students at the same college. This enabled the researcher to judge the verbal accuracy and clarity of the questionnaire items. This also helped to pre-test the questionnaire. Appropriate modifications in the structure and language of the questionnaire items were made based on the lecturers' advice and students' responses.

The questionnaire was appropriate for this particular study in that it allowed respondents to answer items on their own and they had the chance to reflect on issues and carefully consider their responses. The questionnaire is also an objective technique in the sense that it standardizes both questions and responses thus reducing the researcher's subjective tendencies (Oppenheim, 1992). A completed questionnaire ensures that a researcher has at his disposal a permanent record of data collected which he can post-code, analyse at his convenience and refer to as he wishes. Data collected was made easier to analyse through computer analysis. Through its provision for confidentiality by anonymity, the questionnaire can tap more reliable and valid data from student teacher respondents who would otherwise be inhibited by fear to expose their ignorance. By guaranteeing confidentiality of responses it was possible to elicit maximum cooperation from the respondents so that they could expose whatever perceptions they had.

Procedures

The questionnaire was administered to the case study subjects after having secured clearance from the Ministry of Higher Education (see Appendix II). The questionnaire was administered to third year students through the assistance of Mathematics lecturers during lecture hours and collected by the same colleagues. All the questionnaires were administered in March 1997.

Before students completed the questionnaires the researcher explained the purpose of the study and assured them of the confidentiality of their responses, and it was stressed that they should not identify themselves on the questionnaires. A total of 278 questionnaires were collected from the respondents.

Data Analysis

Data collected by questionnaires was analysed through both quantitative and qualitative techniques. In section B of the questionnaire statements positively disposed toward the first year pre-service Mathematics programme were scored 5 for strongly agree, 4 for agree, 3 for undecided, 2 for disagree and 1 for strongly disagree. On the other hand statements which were negatively disposed towards the programme were scored in the reverse direction, that is 1 for strongly agree, 2 for agree, 3 for undecided, 4 for disagree and 5 for strongly disagree. Frequencies, percentages, mean scores and standard deviations were computed for the various groups identified, using the variables in section A (i.e. groupings according to sex, age, teaching experience and subject specialisation). The mean scores for each group of respondents on each item were then classified into five categories according to the following ranges to determine whether each group of respondents agreed or did not agree with each statement on the programme rating scale.

Strongly Agreed	-	4.45 - 5.00
Agreed	-	3.45 - 4.44
Undecided	-	2.45 - 3.44
Disagreed	-	1.45 - 2.44
Strongly Disagreed	-	1.00 - 1.44

For statements that are unfavourably disposed towards the programme, the scale was used in the reverse direction thus:

Strongly Agreed	-	1.00 - 1.44
Agreed	-	1.45 - 2.44
Undecided	-	2.45 - 3.44
Disagreed	-	3.45 - 4.44
Strongly Disagreed	-	4.45 - 5.00

For section C of the questionnaire the frequencies and percentages of the comments made by the respondents were computed after carrying out a content analysis of the responses. The postulated hypotheses were statistically tested using the chi-square test at the level of significance of 0.05. The Epi-info version 6.1 computer programme was used to enter and analyse data.

Summary

This chapter has described the research design, participants, research instruments, procedures and data analysis techniques employed by the researcher. The study now proceeds to the presentation of findings in the next chapter from which discussions, conclusions and recommendations will be made in the final chapter.

CHAPTER 4

RESULTS

Overview

This Chapter presents and analyses data obtained. Analysis also involves relating findings to the study's hypotheses. The results are presented under the following headings:—

Student background characteristics: Respondents' background characteristics of gender, age, Mathematics specialisation and teaching experience were presented.

Overall responses: Respondents' responses on items on subject knowledge, teaching methods, classroom management, resources and teaching personnel were presented and analysed.

Responses by student background characteristics: Responses by student background characteristics of gender, Mathematics specialisation, teaching experience and age were presented and analysed.

Mean scores and standard deviations for various groups: Mean scores and standard deviations for the groups identified by gender, Mathematics specialisation, teaching experience and age were computed for some items.

Major findings: The main findings of the study were outlined and related to the study's hypotheses.

The pre-service Mathematics programme background information: The background information on the structure, content and organisation of the pre-service Mathematics programme was briefly outlined.

Student Background Characteristics

Table 4.1 Frequency table of results of student background characteristics

CHARACTERISTICS	FREQUENCY	%
GENDER		
Male	168	60.4
Female	110	39.6
Total	278	100.0
AGE		
20 - 22 years	81	29.1
23 - 25 years	125	45.0
26 years +	72	25.9
Total	278	100.0
MAIN SUBJECT		
Mathematics	26	9.4
Non-Mathematics	252	90.6
Total	278	100.0
TEACHING EXPERIENCE		
0 years	138	49.6
1 - 3 years	104	37.4
4 years +	27	9.7
Non-response	9	3.2
Total	278	99.9

Table 4.1 shows the frequency distribution of student background characteristics of gender, age, subject specialisation and teaching experience. Of the 278 respondents the majority were males (60.4%). Ages were lumped into three categories to facilitate analysis by chi-square statistics. Most of the respondents (45%) fall in the 23-25 age group.

252 respondents specialise in subjects which are not Mathematics. The intention is to compare views of students in the two categories, namely Mathematics and non-Mathematics. On teaching experience there were 9 non-responses. 138 (49.6%) had no teaching experience. In order to get substantial frequency values analysable by chi-square statistics the years of teaching experience were put into three categories.

Table 4.2.1 Respondents' responses to the items dealing with subject knowledge

BI SUBJECT KNOWLEDGE		SA	A	U	D	SD	NON-Response
i)	There was adequate preparation in Maths content for teaching in primary school during the first year in college	11 4.0%	116 41.7%	23 8.3%	103 37.1%	20 7.2%	5 1.8%
ii)	I had a substantial knowledge base in Maths during teaching practice (TP) to guide and understand pupil's responses	43 15.5%	154 55.4%	32 11.5%	39 14.0%	6 2.2%	4 1.4%
iii)	Some mathematical concepts were difficult to explain during TP	82 29.5%	123 44.2%	8 2.9%	48 17.3%	14 5.0%	3 1.1%
iv)	There was adequate training in the breakdown and sequencing of Maths content for my lessons	36 12.9%	121 43.5%	33 11.9%	65 23.4%	18 6.5%	5 1.8%
v)	It was easy to relate the concepts in Maths to other subjects/areas during teaching.	52 18.7%	141 50.7%	30 10.8%	40 14.4%	9 3.2%	6 2.2%

Key: SA = Strongly Agree; A = Agree; U = Undecided;

D = Disagree; SD = Strongly Disagree

Table 4.2.1 gives responses to the items dealing with subject knowledge. Respondents who gave a "undecided" (U) response were considered together with those who disagreed. Most of the respondents (52.6%) disagreed with the statement that "There was adequate preparation in Maths content for teaching in primary school during the first year in college". 205 (73.7% agreed with the statement "Some mathematical concepts were difficult to explain during TP". However, at least 55% of the respondents favourably agreed with the statements B1 (ii), B1 (iv) and B1 (v).

Table 4.2.2 Respondents' responses to the items dealing with teaching methods

B2 TEACHING METHODS			SA	A	U	D	SA	NON-Response
i)		There was adequate training in the use of the following:						
	a)	Demonstration	83 29.9%	93 33.5%	10 3.6%	65 23.4%	25 9.0%	2 0.7%
	b)	Discussion	52 18.7%	167 60.1%	20 7.2%	24 8.6%	7 2.5%	8 2.9%
	c)	Question and Answer	81 29.1%	136 48.9%	18 6.5%	28 10.1%	7 2.5%	8 2.9%
	d)	Problem Solving	36 12.9%	92 33.1%	29 10.4%	76 27.3%	39 14.0%	6 2.2%
	e)	Discovery	8 2.9%	69 24.8%	36 12.9%	114 41.0%	43 15.5%	8 2.9%
	f)	Brainstorming	9 3.2%	45 16.2%	34 12.2%	78 28.1%	102 36.7%	10 3.6%
ii)	Peer group/micro teaching in the first year helped in TP		71 25.5%	98 35.7%	19 6.8%	31 11.2%	55 19.8%	4 1.4%
iii)	On many occasions I resorted to teaching my pupils in the way I myself was taught Maths at school		53 19.1%	66 23.7%	14 5.0%	92 33.1%	50 18.0%	3 1.1%
iv)	There was adequate training in methods of diagnosing pupil learning difficulties		10 3.6%	42 15.1%	36 12.9%	110 39.6%	78 28.1%	2 0.7%
v)	There was adequate training in the use and preparation of the following instructional materials:							
	a)	Charts	44 15.8%	84 30.2%	15 5.4%	71 25.5%	61 21.9%	3 1.1%
	b)	Models	39 14.0%	99 35.6%	34 12.2%	53 19.1%	49 17.6%	4 1.4%
	c)	Overhead Projector	5 1.8%	4 1.4%	7 2.5%	44 15.8%	214 77.0%	4 1.4%

Table 4.2.2 shows most respondents agreed that there was adequate training in the use of the first three teaching methods, namely the demonstration, discussion and question and answer. According to most of the respondents there was no adequate training in the use of the problem solving, discovery and brainstorming methods. 169 (61.2%) of the respondents considered peer group/micro teaching done in first year to have been helpful during teaching practice. Most of the respondents are of the opinion that there was no adequate training in the use and preparation of charts, models and overhead projector.

Table 4.2.3 Respondents' responses to items dealing with classroom management

B3 CLASSROOM MANAGEMENT		**SA**	**A**	**U**	**D**	**SD**	**NON-Response**
i)	It was difficult to motivate pupils during Maths lessons	9 3.2%	37 13.3%	9 3.2%	138 49.6%	85 30.6%	0 0.0%
ii)	I planned and prepared Maths lessons as we were taught at college	196 70.5%	76 27.3%	1 0.4%	3 1.1%	2 0.7%	0 0.0%
iii)	There was adequate training in formulating lesson objectives	154 55.4%	98 35.3%	9 3.2%	14 5.1%	3 1.1%	0 0.0%
iv)	It was difficult to effectively cater for individual differences in the classroom during Maths lessons	75 27.0%	109 39.2%	18 6.5%	46 16.5%	28 10.1%	2 0.7%
v)	There was adequate training in remedial techniques to enhance pupil understanding of Maths	13 4.7%	20 7.2%	12 4.3%	91 32.7%	140 50.4%	2 0.7%
vi)	There were problems with class discipline during Maths lessons	8 2.9%	54 19.4%	8 2.9%	126 45.3%	80 28.8%	2 0.7%
vii)	Evaluation of Maths lessons was difficult during TP	9 3.2%	15 5.4%	4 1.4%	141 50.7%	107 38.5%	2 0.7%

Table 4.2.3 shows that the highest number of respondents (272) (97.8%) responded positively to the statement "I planned and prepared Maths lessons as we were taught at college". Only 33 (11.9%) of the 278 respondents agreed with the statement "There was adequate training in remedial techniques to enhance pupil understanding of Maths".

Table 4.2.4 Respondents' responses to items dealing with resources and teaching personnel

B4 RESOURCES		**SA**	**A**	**U**	**D**	**SD**	**NON-Response**
i)	There were adequate reading material for Maths assignments	24 8.6%	84 30.2%	27 9.7%	87 31.3%	56 20.1%	0 0.0%
ii)	We were exposed to a variety of equipment for teaching Maths during the first year in college	10 3.6%	38 13.7%	25 9.0%	113 40.6%	88 31.7%	4 1.4%
iii)	More time is needed for teaching Applied Maths during the first year in college	111 39.3%	101 36.3%	24 8.6%	28 10.1%	12 4.3%	2 0.7%
B5 TEACHING PERSONNEL							
i)	There were adequate lecturers for Maths	69 24.8%	127 45.7%	41 14.7%	26 9.4%	14 5.0%	1 0.4%
ii)	Lecturers came well prepared for their lectures	67 24.1%	118 42.4%	60 21.6%	22 7.9%	11 4.0%	0 0.0%
iii)	Lecturers seemed to understand the content they were teaching during Applied Maths lessons	78 28.1%	138 49.6%	48 17.3%	10 3.6%	4 1.4%	0 0.0%
iv)	Lecturers gave relevant examples during lectures	52 18.7%	169 60.8%	19 6.8%	31 11.2%	6 2.2%	1 0.4%
v)	Lecturers made students to feel that Maths teaching was difficult	12 4.3%	24 8.6%	27 9.7%	113 40.6%	102 36.7%	0 0.0%

Table 4.2.4 shows that from most of the respondents' point of view there were inadequate resources and 212 (76.2%) of the respondents are of the view that more time is needed for teaching Applied Maths during the first year in college. The majority of the respondents positively agreed with the statements on the quantity and quality of the teaching personnel. 196 (70.5%) respondents agreed that "there were adequate lecturers for Maths" and 216 (77.7%) were of the opinion that "lecturers seemed to understand the content they were teaching during Applied Maths lessons".

The results of the open ended section C of the questionnaires show that 119 (42.8%) of the respondents indicated that the aspect of the first year pre-service Mathematics programme they liked most was the lectures. Assignments were the aspect disliked most by 106 (38.1%) respondents. Teaching methods were considered the most useful in teaching by 179 (64.4%) respondents. 61 (21.9% of the respondents considered the assignments as the least useful in teaching.

On suggestions on how to improve the programme 75 (27.0%) respondents indicated that micro teaching could be used in preparation for teaching practice. On content coverage in the first year 146 (52.5%) respondents liked more content to be covered. On methods coverage 211 (75.9%) respondents wanted a variety of teaching methods to be taught. On improving the organisation of the programme 103 (37.0%) respondents thought more time was needed for teaching Applied Mathematics.

Responses by student background characteristics

Responses were analysed by student background characteristics of gender, Mathematics specialization, teaching experience and age. The computer package which was used to analyse data automatically computes chi-square values.

Table 4.3.1 Responses by gender to items dealing with subject knowledge

B1 SUBJECT KNOWLEDGE		SA	A	U	D	SD	Non-Response
i) These was adequate preparation in Maths content for teaching in primary school during the first year in college	M	5 3.0%	75 44.4%	14 8.3%	59 35.1%	11 6.5%	4 2.4%
	F	6 5.5%	41 37.3%	9 8.2%	44 40.0%	9 8.2%	1 0.9%
ii) I had a substantial knowledge base in Maths during teaching practice (TP) to guide and understand pupil's responses	M	31 18.5%	95 56.5%	15 8.9%	20 11.9%	4 2.4%	3 1.8%
	F	12 10.9%	59 53.6%	17 15.5%	19 17.3%	2 1.8%	1 0.9%
iii) Som mathematical concepts were difficult to explain during TP	M	43 25.6%	71 42.3%	7 4.2%	34 20.2%	10 6.0%	3 1.8%
	F	39 35.5%	52 47.3%	1 0.9%	14 12.7%	4 3.6%	0 0.0%
iv) There was adequate training in the breakdown and sequencing of Maths content for my lessons	M	23 13.7%	72 42.9%	25 14.9%	30 17.9%	14 8.3%	4 2.4%
	F	13 11.8%	49 44.5%	8 7.3%	35 31.8%	4 3.6%	1 0.9%
v) It was easy to relate the concepts in Maths to other subjects/areas during teaching	M	33 19.6%	75 44.6%	26 15.5%	25 14.9%	5 3.0%	4 2.4%
	F	19 17.3%	66 60.0%	4 3.6%	15 13.6%	4 3.6%	2 1.8%

Note: M is for male and F is for female.

Table 4.3.1 shows respondent's responses by gender to items dealing with subject knowledge. Chi-square analysis of possible association between gender and response was done for all the items on subject knowledge. The computed chi-square (X^2) value for item B1 (iv) produced $X^2 = 11.22 > 9.49$ (4d.f) at 5% level of significance which showed that there were significant differences in responses by respondents of different sex (See Table 4.3 la in Appendix III). For item BI(v) chi-square analysis of response by gender produced $X^2 = 12.07 > 9.49$ (4d.f.) at 5% level of significance which showed that there was a significant relationship (see Table 4.3.1b in Appendix III).

Table 4.3.2 Responses by gender to four of the items dealing with teaching methods

B2 TEACHING METHODS		**SA**	**A**	**U**	**D**	**SD**	**Non-Response**
i) Peer group/micro teaching in the first year helped in TP	M	41 24.4%	54 32.1%	13 7.7%	24 14.3%	32 19.0%	4 2.4%
	F	30 27.3%	44 40.0%	6 5.5%	7 6.4%	23 20.9%	0 0.0%
ii) There was adequate training in the use and preparation of the following instructional materials							
a) Charts	M	28 16.7%	51 30.4%	11 6.5%	40 23.8%	37 22.0%	1 0.6%
	F	16 4.5%	33 30.0%	4 3.6%	31 28.2%	24 21.8%	2 1.8%
b) Models	M	16 9.5%	62 36.9%	22 13.1%	30 17.9%	36 21.4%	2 1.2%
	F	23 20.9%	37 33.6%	12 10.9%	23 20.9%	13 11.8%	2 1.8%
c) Overhead Projector	M	4 2.4%	1 0.6%	4 2.4%	23 13.7%	134 79.8%	2 1.2%
	F	1 0.9%	3 2.7%	3 2.7%	21 19.1%	80 72.7%	2 1.8%

Table 4.3.2 shows responses by gender to four of the items dealing with teaching methods. Table 4.3.2a (See Appendix III) shows that the chi-square analysis of association between gender and response for item B2 (ii) produced $X^2 = 5.68 < 9.49$ (4d.f.) at 5% level of significance. This indicated that there was no significant association between gender and response.

Chi square analysis by gender of item B2 (v) (b) (See Table 4.3.2b in Appendix III) produced $X^2 = 10.42 > 9.49$ (4. d.f.) at 5% level of significance. This shows that there were significant differences in responses between the study subjects of different sex.

Table 4.3.3 Responses by gender to 3 of the items dealing with classroom management

B3 CLASSROOM MANAGEMENT		SA	A	U	D	SD	Non-Response
iii) There was adequate training in formulating lesson objectives	M	102 60.7%	55 32.7%	2 1.2%	7 4.2%	2 1.2%	0 0.0%
	F	52 47.3%	43 39.1%	7 6.4%	7 6.4%	1 0.9%	0 0.0%
iv) It was difficult to effectively cater for individual differences in the classroom during Maths lessons	M	52 31.0%	63 37.5%	11 6.5%	25 14.8%	15 8.9%	2 1.2%
	F	23 2.9%	46 41.8%	7 6.4%	21 19.1%	13 11.8%	0 0.0%
v) There was adequate training in remedial techniques to enhance pupil understanding of Maths	M	6 3.6%	15 8.9%	10 6.1%	45 26.8%	90 53.6%	2 1.2%
	F	7 6.4%	5 4.5%	2 1.8%	46 41.8%	50 45.5%	0 0.0%

Table 4.3.3 shows responses by gender to 3 of the items dealing with classroom management. Chi square analysis of the possible association between gender and response for item B3 (iii) produced $X^2 = 9.11 < 9.49$ (4 d.f.) at 0.05 level of significance which showed no significant relationship (See Appendix III Table 4.3.3a). A similar chi-square analysis for item B3 (v) produced $X^2 = 10.94 > 9.49$ (4d.f.) at 0.05 level of significance. (See Appendix III Table 4.3.3b). This showed that there were significant differences in responses by respondents of different sex.

Table 4.3.4 Responses by Maths specialisation

B1 SUBJECT KNOWLEDGE		SA	A	U	D	SD	Non-Response
i) Some mathematical concepts were difficult to explain during TP	Maths	6 23.1%	9 34.6%	1 3.8%	6 23.1%	4 15.4%	0 0.0%
	Non-Maths	76 30.2%	114 45.2%	7 2.8%	42 16.7%	10 4.0%	3 1.2%
ii) There was adequate training in the breakdown and sequencing of Maths content for my lessons	Maths	6 23.1%	8 30.8%	6 23.1%	3 23.1%	0 0.0%	0 0.0%
	Non-Maths	30 11.9%	113 44.8%	27 10.7%	59 23.4%	18 7.1%	5 2.0%
B2 TEACHING METHODS							
i) There was adequate training in the use of the following: c) Discovery	Maths	0 0.0%	1 3.8%	3 11.5%	13 50.0%	8 30.8%	1 3.8%
	Non-Maths	8 3.8%	68 27.0%	33 13.1%	101 40.1%	35 13.9%	7 2.8%
B5 TEACHING PERSONNEL							
ii) Lecturers gave relevant examples during lectures	Maths	6 23.1%	12 46.2%	1 3.8%	7 26.9%	0 0.0%	0 0.0%
	Non-Maths	46 18.3%	157 62.5%	18 7.2%	24 9.6%	6 2.4%	1 0.4%

Table 4.3.4 shows responses by Mathematics specialisation. All respondents whose main subject is not Mathematics are grouped in the "Non-Maths" category. A statistical analysis was done to find if there were significant differences in the responses of those who specialise in Mathematics and those who do not major in Mathematics. Chi-square analysis by Mathematics specialisation of item B1 (iii) produced $X^2 = 7.68 < 9.49$ (4 d.f.) at 5% level of significance (see Appendix III Table 4.3.4a). This shows that there were no significant differences in responses between Mathematics specialists and those who specialise in other subjects.

A similar chi-square analysis for item B1 (iv) produced $X^2 = 8.09 < 9.49$ (4 d.f.) at 5% level of significance (see Appendix III Table 4.3.4b). This indicated that there was no significant association between Mathematics specialisation and response. However significant differences in responses by Mathematics specialisation was found for item B2 (i) (e) as the chi-square analysis produced $X^2 = 10.96 > 9.49$ (4 d.f.) at 5% level of significance (see Appendix III Table 4.3.4c). No significant differences in responses by Mathematics specialisation was found for item B5 (iv) whose chi-square analysis produced $X^2 = 8.67 < 9.49$ (4 d.f.) at 0.05 level of significance (see Appendix III Table 4.3.4d).

Table 4.3.5 Responses by teaching experience

B2 TEACHING METHODS	Exp	SA	A	U	D	SD	Non-Response
ii) Peer group/microteaching in the first year helped in TP	0	45 32.6%	48 34.8%	10 7.2%	12 8.7%	23 16.7%	0 0.0%
	1 - 3	19 18.3%	41 39.4%	6 5.8%	11 10.6%	24 23.1%	3 2.9%
	4 +	4 14.8%	8 29.6%	2 7.4%	7 25.9%	6 22.2%	0 0.0%
B3 CLASSROOM MANAGEMENT							
iv) It was difficult to effectively cater for individual differences in the classroom during Maths lessons	0	38 27.5%	58 42.0%	11 8.0%	19 13.8%	11 8.0%	1 1.0%
	1 - 3	28 26.9%	40 38.5%	5 4.8%	20 19.2%	10 9.6%	1 1.0%
	4 +	6 22.2%	10 37.0%	1 3.7%	3 11.1%	7 25.9%	0 0.0%
B5 TEACHING PERSONNEL							
iv) Lecturers gave relevant examples during lectures	0	23 16.7%	89 64.5%	7 6.1%	15 10.9%	3 2.2%	1 0.7%
	1 - 3	22 21.2%	60 57.7%	7 6.7%	14 13.5%	1 1.0%	0 0.0%
	4 +	5 18.5%	14 51.9%	5 18.5%	2 7.4%	1 3.7%	0 0.0%

Note: Exp. = Teaching Experience (in years)

Number of missing observations: 9

Table 4.3.5 shows respondents' responses by teaching experience prior to joining college to some items dealing with teaching methods, classroom management and teaching personnel. Chi-square analysis of the possible association between teaching experience and response for item B2 (ii) produced $X^2 = 14.31 < 15.51$ (8 d.f.) at 5% level of significance which showed no significant relationship (see Appendix III Table 4.3.4a).

Chi-square analysis for item B3 (iv) produced $X^2 = 10.33 < 15.51$ (8d.f) at 0.05 level of significance (see Appendix III Table 4.3.5b). This shows that there were no significant differences in responses among the respondents of different years of teaching experience. A similar result was obtained for item B5 (iv) with $X^2 = 9.06 < 15.51$ (8d.f.) at 5% level of significance (see Appendix III Table 4.3.5c).

In Table 4.3.5 above more than half of the respondents in each of the three categories of teaching experience are agreeing with each of the statements. For the last item B5 ;(iv) at least 70% of the respondents in each category are in agreement with the statement "Lecturers gave relevant examples during lectures".

Table 4.3.6 Responses by age

B5 TEACHING PERSONNEL	Age	SA	A	U	D	SD	Non-Response
i) There were adequate lecturers for Maths	20-22	23 28.4%	34 42.0%	9 11.1%	8 9.9%	7 8.6%	0 0.0%
	23-25	30 24.0%	65 52.0%	16 12.0%	8 6.4%	6 4.8%	0 0.0%
	26 +	16 22.2%	28 38.9%	17 23.6%	10 13.9%	1 1.4%	0 0.0%
iii) Lecturers seemed to understand the content they were teaching during Applied Maths Lessons	20-22	16 19.8%	47 58.0%	14 17.3%	4 4.9%	0 0.0%	0 0.0%
	23-25	40 32.0%	57 45.6%	23 18.4%	4 3.2%	1 0.8%	0 0.0%
	26 +	22 30.6%	34 47.2%	11 15.3%	2 2.8%	3 4.2%	0 0.0%
iv) Lecturers gave relevant examples during lectures	20-22	7 8.6%	64 79.0%	1 1.2%	9 11.1%	0 0.0%	0 0.0%
	23-25	32 25.6%	64 51.2%	9 7.2%	14 11.2%	5 4.0%	1 0.8%
	26 +	13 18.1%	41 56.9%	9 12.5%	8 11.1%	1 1.4%	0 0.0%

Table 4.3.6 shows responses by age to three of the items dealing with teaching personnel. A chi-square analysis was done to find if there were significant differences in the responses by age groups. For item B5 (i) the computed $X^2 = 14.66 < 15.51$ (8d.f.) at 0.05 level of significance (see Appendix III Table 4.3.6a) shows that there were no significant differences in responses among the three age groups. A similar statistical analysis for item B5 (iii) produced $X^2 = 10.58 < 15.51$ (8d.f) at 0.05 level of significance (see Appendix III Table 4.3.6b). This indicates that there were no significant differences in responses by age. However significant differences in responses by age were noted for item B5 (iv). The chi-square analysis produced $X^2 = 25.06 > 15.51$ (8d.f.) at 5% level of significance (see Table 4.3.6c in Appendix III).

Mean scores and standard deviations for the various groups

Men scores and standard deviations were computed for the various groups identified on the basis of the independent variables in Section A of the questionnaire. The computer was used to compute the mean scores and standard deviations.

Table 4.3.7 Mean scores and standard deviations for the various groups for B3 (ii)

Statement	Variable		Mean	Standard deviation
B3 (ii) I planned and prepared Maths lessons as we were taught at college	*Gender*			
	Males		4.6726	0.6428
	Females		4.6364	0.5862
	Teaching Experience (Yrs)			
		0	4.7101	0.5564
		1 - 3	4.6214	0.6435
		4 +	4.6670	0.4804
	Age (Years):	20 - 22	4.6420	0.5768
		24 - 25	4.6480	0.7213
		26 +	4.6944	0.4639
	Main Subject:	Maths	4.6538	0.4852
		Non-Maths	4.6587	0.6332

Table 4.3.7 shows the mean scores and standard deviations for the various groups of gender, teaching experience, age and Mathematics specialisation. The means for all the groups are within the range 4.45 to 5.00. This means all the groups strongly agree with the statement "I planned and prepared Maths lessons as we were taught at college". The standard deviations are fairly small (<0.73). This show the responses are almost the same within each group.

Table 4.3.8 Mean scores and standard deviations for the various groups for B3 (v)

Statement	Variable		Mean	Standard deviation
B3 (v) There was adequate training in remedial techniques to enhance pupil understanding of Maths	*Gender*			
	Males		1.8072	1.1223
	Females		1.8450	1.1020
	Teaching Experience (Yrs)			
		0	1.8529	1.0990
		1 - 3	1.6731	0.9940
		4 +	1.9630	1.2850
	Age (Years):	20 - 22	1.6750	0.9520
		24 - 25	1.8870	1.1840
		26 +	1.8750	1.1500
	Main Subject:	Maths	1.3460	0.5620
		Non-Maths	1.8720	1.1441

The mean scores and standard deviations for various groups are shown in Table 4.3.8. All the groups except those whom main subject is Mathematics have means within the range 1.45 to 2.44 which means they disagree with the statement B3 (v). The Mathematics specialists with a mean of 1.3460 strongly disagree with the statement and the standard deviation of 0.562 shows that their responses are not very varied.

Mean scores and standard deviations for all the items for which chi-square analysis was done to find the possible association between the independent variables (of gender, Mathematics specialisation, teaching experience and age) and the dependent variable 'students' perceptions of the pre-service Mathematics programme' (reflected in responses to the questionnaire) are shown in Appendix III.

Major Findings

The following are the major findings of this study:

1) Students favourably agreed with statements on the adequacy of preparation of teaching mathematical knowledge.

2) Students felt that more teaching methods could be covered.

3) Micro-teaching was considered helpful in teaching practice.

4) Students believed that training in the use and preparation of instructional materials was inadequate.

5) Students planned and prepared Mathematics lessons as they were taught at college.

6) Students were inadequately trained in remedial techniques to enhance pupils' understanding of Mathematics.

7) Students would like to see improvement in the availability of resources for teaching Applied Mathematics.

8) Students favourably agreed with statements on the quality and quantity of teaching personnel.

9) Data from the unstructured section of the questionnaire suggests that assignments could be made more relevant to teaching and micro-teaching could be used in preparation for teaching practice.

10)(i) There were significant differences in responses by gender to the following statements:

a) "There was adequate training in the breakdown and sequencing of Maths content for my lessons". Mean scores for males and females were 3.3659 and 3.294 respectively.

b) "It was easy to relate the concepts in Maths to other subjects/areas during teaching". Females had a higher mean score (3.75) than males (3.6463).

c) "There was adequate training in the use and preparation of models". Females had a mean score of 3.315 and that of males was 2.952.

d) "There was adequate training in remedial techniques to enhance pupil understanding of Maths". The respective mean scores for males and females were 1.8072 and 1.8450.

10)(ii) Chi-square analysis of the possible association between the independent variable 'gender' and the dependent variable 'students' perceptions of the pre-service Mathematics programme' (reflected in responses to the questionnaire) indicated a significant relationship for the statements in 10 (i) (a) to (d) (See Appendix III Tables 4.3.1a, 4.3.1b, 4.3.2b and 4.3.3b). For these statements the null hypothesis 'Gender has no effect on students perceptions of the pre-service Mathematics programme' was rejected.

11) There were significant differences in responses by Mathematics specialisation to the statement "There was adequate training in the use of the discovery method". Mathematics specialists scored a mean of 1.8800 and the non-Mathematics specialists had a mean score of 2.6449. Chi-square analysis led to the rejection of the null hypothesis 'Mathematics specialisation has no effect on students' perceptions of the pre-service Mathematics programme' for this particular statement (see Appendix III Table 4.3.3c).

12) There were significant differences in responses by age to the statement "Lecturers gave relevant examples during lectures". The three age groups of 20 - 22 years, 23 - 25 y ears and 26 + years had mean scores of 3.8519, 3.8387 and 3.7920 respectively. Chi-square analysis for this statement indicated a significant relationship between the independent variable 'age' and the dependent variable 'students' perceptions of the pre-service Mathematics programme' (reflected in responses to the questionnaire). As a result the null hypothesis 'Age has no effect on students' perceptions of the pre-service Mathematics programme' was rejected for this particular statement (see Appendix III Table 4.3.6c).

13) There were no significant differences in responses by teaching experience to all the statements on subject knowledge, teaching methods, classroom management, resources and teaching personnel. Chi-square analysis of the possible association between the variables of teaching experience and students' perceptions of the pre-service Mathematics programme (reflected in responses to the questionnaire) indicated no significant relationship (see Appendix III Tables 4.3.5a, 4.3.5b and 4.3.5c). This means the null hypothesis 'Teaching experience prior to training has no effect on students' perceptions of the pre-service Mathematics programme' was retained.

These major findings of this study will be discussed in the next chapter within the context of the pre-service Mathematics programme background information.

The Pre-service Mathematics Programme Background Information

Seke Teachers' College is a government institution which was established in 1980. The college trains pre-service and in-service primary school teachers. It has an enrollment of 1377 students in 1977 and a lecturing staff of 65. Like other non-graduate primary teachers' college in Zimbabwe, Seke Teachers' College is an associate college of the University of Zimbabwe (UZ) through the Department of Teacher Education (DTE). The associateship status of the college means that entry qualifications, general regulations, curriculum followed and diplomas awarded to successful candidates are approved by the UZ (Chivore, 1994).

The pre-service students can be grouped into two groups, namely the infant Diploma in Education and the general Diploma in Education courses. As this study is focused on the pre-service Mathematics programme of those following the general Diploma in Education (DE) course this discussion now focuses on the details of this particular course.

The general DE course has four sections and the student has to pass each of these. Teaching Practice is Section I, Theory of Education is Section II, Main Subject is Section III and Professional Studies in Section IV. The Professional Studies comprises of Syllabuses A, B and C and Co-curricular studies. Syllabus A is on the general methods of teaching. Syllabus B is made up of Applied Education Subjects. Applied Education Subjects are Mathematics, English, Shona, Environmental Science, Social Studies, Music, Physical Education, Religious and Moral Education (RME), Home Economics and Art and Craft. Applied Education relates to those subjects more closely related to classroom practice in the primary school. Educational Technology and Health Education are the two Co-curricular studies although there are moves at the moment to make them Applied Education subjects. Syllabus C is the Curriculum Depth Study (CDS).

The pre-service Mathematics programme includes Mathematics Applied Education, Mathematics Main Subject and Mathematics CDS. In Mathematics Applied Education (commonly known as Applied Mathematics) the focus is on the philosophy of the subject, methods of teaching, enrichment component, preparation for teaching, assessment and general theories of how children learn the subject. In Mathematics Main Subject students study to advance their academic content knowledge in the subject to a level beyond Ordinary Level and for some topics slightly beyond Advanced Level. A student has to choose one Main Subject and as a result only about thirty students major in Mathematics in each year group. In Mathematics CDS students carry out a classroom based research as a way of trying to marry theory and practice in the process of teaching. Only a few (about 30) opt for this component in each year group.

For Applied Education lectures the students are divided into three groups of about one hundred students. The applied subjects are paired, for example Mathematics is paired with Environmental Science, and two-hour lectures are conducted on alternating weeks. One lecturer takes the whole group for the two-hour lecture. Main Subject has two hours and four hours per week for first and third years respectively. For the first years the single two-hour block is shared by two lecturers. The two two-hour blocks for the third years are shared among four lecturers. The CDS introductory lectures are mass lectures conducted by the four Syllabus A lecturers. After the introductory lectures students choose their CDS subject areas. The first six lectures for the Mathematics CDS group are conducted for the whole group for two hours every week. After these lectures students are assigned to supervisors. The supervisors conduct tutorials and consultations for students in their respective groups up to third year.

There are four lecturers in the Mathematics Department. All the lecturers have at least a first degree and majored in Mathematics. Before being promoted to lectureship the lecturers had taught in secondary schools. The lecturers teach the Mathematics Applied Education on a rotational basis. For Mathematics Main Subject the lecturers teach different topics in different one-hour slots. A lecturer supervises about eight students in each year group in CDS research projects.

Students are assessed by way of three assignments in Mathematics Applied Education and are expected to obtain an overall pass of 50% or better. However one of the requirements for passing Section IV is that they should pass in at least seven Applied Education areas which mean that one can afford to fail three areas and still pass. The CDS research project which is part of Section IV has to be passed at 50% or better. In Mathematics Main Subject students are assessed by way of at least five unit tests and two history of Mathematics essays for the coursework component. The second component is an examination in which students write two two-and-half hour papers. Each of these two components has to be passed by obtaining a mark of at least 50%.

CHAPTER 5

DISCUSSION, CONCLUSIONS AND RECOMMENDATIONS

This study sought to investigate third year student teachers' perceptions of the first year pre-service Mathematics programme. The study also sought to find out whether student background characteristics of gender, age, teaching experience and Mathematics specialisation had any effect on students' perceptions of the pre-service Mathematics programme. College inputs and processes which could be improved were also investigated.

This chapter discusses the findings and makes the conclusions and recommendations based on the results.

Discussion

Respondents in this study are of the view that some preparation in subject knowledge was done in the first year in college. Preparation in subject knowledge has received a lot of support from those who have contributed to the debate on how best to educate teachers (Shulman, 1986; Ernest, 1989; Igboko, 1976). Fennema, Carpenter and Peterson (1992) have even argued that teachers need in-depth knowledge not only of the specific mathematics they teach, but also of the mathematics that their students are to learn in future. In this study those who specialise in Mathematics were expected to give different responses on items on subject knowledge from those who do not major in Mathematics. However no significant differences in responses on these items between the Mathematics specialists and the non-Mathematics specialists were noted in this study. In the absence of other research findings in this area, the results may only be validated by further studies especially replicated studies not only involving different student teacher year groups, but other teacher training colleges in Zimbabwe.

This study has showed that more could be done on methods of teaching, use of instructional materials and remedial techniques to enhance pupil understanding of mathematical concepts. These findings are supported by Morris and Stones (1972), Watts (1982) and Shumba (1991). For example, Shumba (1991)'s study revealed that student teachers had major shortfalls in planning lessons which include problems of sequencing, lack of reference to teaching aids, poor evaluations and failure to make provision for slow learners. Shumba (1991) even went further to suggest that 'these were all weaknesses which colleges can remedy during pre-service training' (p. 9). The students' shortcomings mentioned by Shumba (1991) are some of the professional skills which lie at the heart of the training process (Proctor, 1984) which teachers' colleges could address. One way colleges could improve students' professional skills is by improving the provision of resources like time and reading materials which students cited as inadequate for the pre-service Mathematics programme. For example, the one hour per week for Applied Mathematics lectures could hardly be considered adequate to prepare students to teach a core subject like Mathematics in the primary school.

Some of the ways suggested for improving the pre-service Mathematics programme were to make use of more micro-teaching in preparation for teaching and giving practical assignments which are relevant to teaching. Although it seems there are no previous studies which actually investigated what can be done to improve a pre-service Mathematics programme, this study's findings are never the less supported by other studies on ways of improving methods of training teachers. Pauline (1993) found micro teaching to be an efficient way to teach students in method classes. Watts (1982) called on colleges of education to address the 'practitioners' needs' to adequately prepare students for the hard task of teaching. For example, practical assignments on classroom managerial skills could benefit the students more than those on writing hypothetical schemes of work and lesson plans.

Significant differences in responses by gender to two items on subject knowledge, one on teaching methods and one on classroom management were observed in this study in which students' perceptions of the pre-service Mathematics programme were reflected in responses to the questionnaire. In three of these four responses females had higher mean scores than males. This finding could be consistent with the findings of Akpe (1988) who carried out an evaluation of a Nigerian college education programme using students' perceptions of the programme and found that female students seemed more satisfied with the programme than their male counterparts.

Using the independent variables of Mathematics specialisation and age, only one significant difference in response for each was noted in this study. One is likely to say that the possible relationship between the independent variables and responses was indicated in too few items to warrant a definite conclusion. This certainly requires further investigation. The present writer did not come across research findings which could shed more light on these particular findings at the time of carrying this study. The other interesting finding of this study was that there was no relationship between the independent variable 'teaching experience' and students' perceptions of the pre-service Mathematics programme. One was likely to assume that student teachers exposed to teaching prior to joining college are likely to have different perceptions of the pre-service Mathematics programme from those without teaching experience. However this finding needs to be validated by further studies especially by those of a longitudinal nature.

Conclusions

Findings from the study were that students were of the view that although the pre-service Mathematics programme was able to give them a foundation in subject knowledge there is room for improvement in training in teaching methods, classroom management and provision of resources. Students were satisfied with the quality and quantity of teaching personnel. The study showed that gender had an effect on students' perceptions of the pre-service Mathematics programme. Females seemed more satisfied with the pre-service Mathematics programme than their male counterparts in the cases where there were significant differences in responses. The study also revealed that Mathematics specialisation that an effect on students' perception of the programme as regards the use of the discovery method only. Age also had an effect on students' perception of the programme's teaching personnel's use of examples during lectures only. It was concluded from this study that students had the same perceptions of the pre-service Mathematics programme regardless of years of teaching experience prior to joining college.

Recommendations

In the light of the research problem, the findings presented in chapter four and the conclusions, the researcher wishes to make the following recommendations for practice and future research.

1. There is need for the college to step up training in the use of teaching methods, instructional material sand remediation techniques in Mathematics.

2. More micro teaching sessions should be carried out with students in preparation for teaching.

3. The college needs more time for teaching Mathematics which is a core subject in the primary school. There is no justification for Mathematics to have the same time as other non-core subjects in the primary school. Clustering of subjects can be considered as a way of creating more time for the core subjects.

4. Future research can investigate the effect of other variables like teaching practice school characteristics and the student's performance on teaching practice which were not investigated in this study on the students' perception of the pre-service Mathematics programme.

5. There is need to replicate this study using a wider sample to be drawn from all primary teachers' colleges in Zimbabwe. It is hoped that a replication study will shed more light on the seemingly grey areas of this study like the effect of age and Mathematics specialisation on students' perceptions of the pre-service Mathematics programme.

REFERENCES

Akpe, C. (1988) Using Consumer Evaluation to Improve College Curriculum in Nigerian Teacher Training. *Journal of Education for Teaching, 14* (1), 85 - 90.

Brown, S., Cooney, T. and Jones, D. (1992) Teachers' Knowledge and Its Impact. In D. Grouws (Ed), *Handbook of Research on Mathematics Teaching and Learning*. New York: Macmillan.

Brown, R. and Brown, D. (1992) *Curriculum and Instruction*. London. Macmillan.

Carr, W. and Kemmis, S. (1986) *Becoming Critical: Education, Knowledge and Action Research*. London: Falmer Press.

Chawanji, D. (1992) An examination of the Perceptions of Third Year Student Teachers and Lecturers on Teacher Education and Training Practices at Belvedere Technical Teachers' College: An Application of Critical Theory in the Analysis of Educational Discourse in Teacher Education. Unpublished M.Ed dissertation, University of Zimbabwe, Harare.

Chihaka, T. (1994) An investigation into the effect of students' background characteristics, teaching school characteristics, college inputs and processes on Belvedere Technical Teachers' College Mathematics Students' teaching practice performance. Unpublished M.Sc. Mathematics Education dissertation, University of Zimbabwe, Harare.

Chivore, B. (1991) *Curriculum Evaluation in Zimbabwe: An Appraisal of Case Studies*. Harare: Books for Africa.

Chivore, B. (1994) *The Effectiveness of the Primary School Teacher in Zimbabwe*. Gweru: Mambo Press.

Choppin, B. (1977) The use of tests and scales in curriculum evaluation. In A. Lewy (Ed), *Handbook of Evaluation*, p. 229.

Cohen, L. and Manion, L. (1977) *A Guide to Teaching Practice*. London: Methuen and Company.

Costin, F., Greenough, W. and Monges, R. (1971)

Student Ratings of College Teaching: Reliability, Validity and Usefulness. *Review of Educational Research, 41*, 511-535.

Darley, M., Glucksberg, S., Kamin, L. and Kinchla, R. (1981)

Psychology, 2nd Edition. New Jersey: Prentice Hall.

DeCecco, J. (1968) *The Psychology of Learning and Instruction: Educational Psychology*. New Jersey: Prentice Hall.

Dubey, D. (1986) *Teaching in the Primary School*. London: Longman.

Dunkin, M. and Barnes, J. (1986) Research on Teaching Higher Education. In M. Wittrock (Ed), *Handbook of Research on Teaching* 3rd Edition. (pp. 754 - 776). New York: Macmillan.

Elbaz, F. (1983) *Teacher Thinking: A study of practical knowledge*. New York: Nichols.

Elliot, J. (1989) Educational Theory and the professional learning of teachers. *Cambridge Journal of Education, 19* (1), 81-101.

Ernest, P. (1989) The Knowledge, Beliefs and Attitudes of the Mathematics teacher: A Model. *Journal of Education for Teaching, 15* (1), 13 - 33.

Farrant, J. (1981) *Principles and Practice of Education*. London: Longman.

Fennema, E., Carpenter, T. and Peterson, P. (1992)

Teachers' Knowledge and Its Impact. In D. Grouws (Ed), *Handbook of Research on Mathematics Teaching and Learning*. New York: Macmillan.

Griffiths, M. and Tann, S. (1992) Using Reflective Practice to Link personal and Public Theories. *Journal of Education for Teaching, 18* (1), 69 - 85.

Grossman, P., Wilson, S. and Shulman, L. (1989)

Teachers of Substance: subject matter knowledge for teaching. In M. Reynolds (Ed), *Knowledge Base for the Beginning Teacher*, pp. 23 - 36. Oxford: Pergamon Press.

Igboko, P. (1976) Basic Mathematics for the UPE Teacher. *West African Journal of Education, XX* (1).

Isaac, S. and Michael, B. (1984) *Handbook In Research and Evaluation*, California: Edits Publishers.

Kasanda, C. (1992) The Zambia Mathematics Pre-Service Programme: Its Ability To Impart Teaching Strategies And Classroom Management Skills As Perceived By Its Graduates. *Zimbabwe Journal of Educational Research, 4* (3), 285 - 293.

Louw, D. and Edwards, D. (1993) *Psychology: An Introduction for Students in Southern Africa*. Johnannesburg: Lexicon.

Luft, J. (1969) *Human Interaction*. California: Mayfield Publishing.

McCullough, L. and Mintz, S. (1992)

Concerns of Pre-Service Students in the USA about the Practice of Teaching. *Journal of Education for Teaching, 18* (1), 59 - 67.

McKeachie, W. (1979) Student ratings of faculty. *Academy, 65*, 384 - 397.

McNamara, D. (1990) Research on Teachers' thinking: its contribution to educating student teachers to think critically. *Journal of Education for Teaching, 16*, 147 - 160.

Menges, R. (1979) Evaluating teaching effectiveness: What is the proper role of students? *Liberal Education, 65*, 356 - 370.

Meredith, A. (1993) Knowledge for teaching Mathematics: some student teachers' views. *Journal of Education for Teaching, 19* (3), 325 - 338).

Morris, E. and Stones, E. (1972) *Teaching Practice: Problems and Perspectives: A Reappraisal of the Practical Professional Elements in Teacher Preparation*. Longon: Methuen.

Morrison, E. and McIntyre, D. (1969) *Teachers and Teaching*. Middlesex: Penguin.

Nyikahadzoyi, M. (1994) A Comparison of attitudes of first and third year student teachers towards college Mathematics and the teaching of Mathematics: A Case Study of Morgenster Teachers' College. Unpublished M.Sc. Mathematics Education dissertation, University of Zimbabwe, Harare.

Oppenheim, A. (1992) *Questionnaire Design, Interviewing and Attitude Measurement*. (New Ed). London: Printer Publishers.

Pauline, R. (1993) Microteaching. *Journal of Science Education, 4* (1), 9 - 17.

Proctor, N. (1984) Professional Studies and the QTS Review. *Journal of Education for Teaching, 10* (1), 61 - 72.

Schon, D. (1983) *The Reflective Practitioiner*. London: Temple Smith.

Shulman, L. (1986) Paradigms and research programs in the study of teaching: a contemporary perspective. In M. Wittrock, *Third Handbook of Research on Teaching*, pp. 3 - 36, New York, Macmillan.

Shulman, L. (1987) Knowledge and Teaching: Foundations of the new reform. *Harvard Educational Review, 57*, 1 - 22.

Shumba, O. (1991) TP: An Overview of the Findings of External Assessors. *The Zimbabwe Bulletin of Teacher Education, 1* (1), 1 - 33.

Stones, E. (1989) Pedagogical studies in the theory and practice of teacher education. *Oxford Review of Education, 15*, 3 - 15.

Watts, D. (1982) Can Campus-Based Pre-Service Teacher Education Survive? *Journal of Teacher Education, XXXIII* (2), 37 - 41.

Wehmeier, S. (Ed). (1991) *Oxford Wordpower Dictionary*. Oxford: Oxford University Press.

Windham, D. (1988) *Indicators of Educational Effectiveness and Efficiency.* New York: University Press.

Wittrock, M. (Ed). (1986) *Handbook of Research on Teaching*, 3rd Edition. New York: Macmillan.

World Bank (1988) *Education in Sub-Saharan Africa: Policies for Adjustment, Revitalisation and Expansion.* Washington, D.C.: World Bank.

Zeichner, K. and Liston, D. (1987) Teaching Student Teachers to Reflect. *Harvard Educational Review, 57* (1), 23 - 45.

APPENDIX I

UNIVERSITY OF ZIMBABWE

DEPARTMENT OF TEACHER EDUCATION

STUDENT TEACHERS' PERCEPTIONS QUESTIONNAIRE

Dear Sir/Madam

This questionnaire is designed to find out student teachers' perceptions of the first year pre-service Mathematics programme's ability to impart teaching strategies and classroom management skills to trainee teachers. Since there is no right or wrong answer in assessing people's perceptions, please answer as frankly as possible each of the items on this questionnaire. Your responses are confidential and will be used solely for the purposes of this study.

SECTION A: STUDENT BACKGROUND CHARACTERISTICS

Complete the following:

A1 Sex (Gender) . . . .
A2 Age (in years) . . . .
A3 Main Subject . . . .
A4 Previous teaching experience prior to joining college (in years) . . . .

SECTION B: COLLEGE INPUTS AND PROCESSES

Respond to the following series of statements about the first year pre-service Mathematics programme. ***PLEASE CIRCLE THE APPROPRIATE SCORE*** in one of the columns at the right hand side to show whether you:

Strongly Agree (SA) = 5; Agree (A) = 4; Undecided (U) = 3; Disagree (D) = 2; or Strongly Disagree (SD) = 1.

B1 SUBJECT KNOWLEDGE	SA	A	U	D	SD
i) There was adequate preparation in Maths content for teaching in primary school during the first year in college	5	4	3	2	1
ii) I had a substantial knowledge base in Maths during teaching practice (TP) to guide and understand pupil's responses.	5	4	3	2	1
iii) Some mathematical concepts were difficult to explain during TP.	5	4	3	2	1
iv) There was adequate training in the breakdown and sequencing of Maths content for my lessons	5	4	3	2	1
v) It was easy to relate the concepts in Maths to other subjects/ areas during teaching.	5	4	3	2	1
B2 TEACHING METHODS					
i) There was adequate training in the use of the following:					
a) Demonstration	5	4	3	2	1
b) Discussion	5	4	3	2	1
c) Question and Answer	5	4	3	2	1
d) Problem Solving	5	4	3	2	1
e) Discovery	5	4	3	2	1
f) Brainstorming	5	4	3	2	1
ii) Peer group/micro teaching in the first year helped in TP.	5	4	3	2	1
iii) On many occasions I resorted to teaching my pupils in the way I myself was taught Maths at school	5	4	3	2	1
iv) There was adequate training in methods of diagnosing pupil learning difficulties.	5	4	3	2	1
v) There was adequate training in the use and preparation of the following instructional materials:	5	4	3	2	1
	5	4	3	2	1
a) Charts	5	4	3	2	1
b) Models	5	4	3	2	1
c) Overhead Projector					
d) Other (specify)					

B3 CLASSROOM MANAGEMENT	SA	A	U	D	SD
i) It was difficult to motivate pupils during Maths lessons.	5	4	3	2	1
ii) I planned and prepared Maths lessons as we were taught at college.	5	4	3	2	1
iii) There was adequate training in formulating lesson objectives.	5	4	3	2	1
iv) It was difficult to effectively cater for individual differences in the classroom during Maths lessons.	5	4	3	2	1
v) There was adequate training in remedial techniques to enhance pupil understanding of Maths.	5	4	3	2	1
vi) There were problems with class discipline during Maths lessons.	5	4	3	2	1
vii) Evaluation of Maths lessons was difficult during TP.	5	4	3	2	1
B3 RESOURCES					
i) There were adequate reading materials for Maths assignments	5	4	3	2	1
ii) We were exposed to a variety of equipment for teaching Maths during the first year in college.	5	4	3	2	1
iii) More time is needed for teaching Applied Maths during the first year in college.	5	4	3	2	1
B5 TEACHING PERSONNEL					
i) There were adequate lecturers for Maths.	5	4	3	2	1
ii) Lecturers came well prepared for their lectures.	5	4	3	2	1
iii) Lecturers seemed to understand the content they were teaching during Applied Maths Lessons	5	4	3	2	1
iv) Lecturers gave relent examples during lectures.	5	4	3	2	1
v) Lecturers made students to feel that Maths teaching was difficult.	5	4	3	2	1

SECTION C: STUDENT OBSERVATIONS

C1 Indicate the aspects of the First Year pre-service Mathematics programme you:

i) Like most

....

....

ii) Disliked most

....

....

iii) Considered most useful in teaching

....

....

iv) Considered least useful

....

....

C2 Write down your suggestions on how each of the following can be improved in the first year pre-service Mathematics programme.

i) Preparation for teaching practice

....

....

ii) Content coverage in the first year.

....

....

iii) Methods coverage in the first year.

....

....

iv) Organisation of the programme

....

....

v) Any other aspect (specify)

....

....

APPENDIX II

27 January, 1997

The Chairman
Department of Teacher Education
University of Zimbabwe
P O Box MP 167
Harare

re: *APPLICATION FOR RESEARCH IN TEACHER COLLEGES—M ED STUDENTS 1997*

The following students have been cleared to conduct research in teacher colleges:

CHABAYA OWENCE: Affirmative action in Teachers Colleges.	GTC
MASVIMBO ASEAL: The Effects of Socialisation Patterns in the Academic Performance of Student Teachers.	GTC
CHISUNGA CHRISTOPHER: The Nature of Problem Solving in Mechanical Engineering Department at Chinhoyi Technical Teachers College.	CHINHOYI
MASHIPE EVERISTO: A Case Study into the Mentors Roles and Mentors Attitudes Towards the New Attachment System of TP in the Midlands Province of Zimbabwe.	
MUYENGWA BANARRAS: An Investigation into Ability of The Pre-service Maths Programme at Seke Teachers College to Impact Classroom & Teaching Strategies as Perceived by Students.	SEKE

For future applications, we would need more information about the institutions at which the research is to be conducted and the methodology of research e.g. questionnaires or interviews.

J Nyamhetsi (Mr)
For Secretary for Higher Education

APPENDIX III

COMPUTATIONS OF CHI-SQUARE VALUES FOR ASSOCIATION BETWEEN RESPONSES TO SOME STATEMENTS AND STUDENT BACKGROUND CHARACTERISTICS (OF GENDER, AGE, MAIN SUBJECT AND TEACHING EXPERIENCE).

The computer programme which was used to enter and analyse data automatically computes chi-square (X^2) values. Item numbers correspond with the numbering in the questionnaire.

Table 4.3.1a Relationship between gender and response to item B1 (iv)

H_0: There is no relationship between gender and response to B1 (vi)

H_1: There is a relationship between gender and response to B1 (iv)

GENDER	RESPONSES						Mean Score	S.D
	SA	A	U	D	SD	Total		
Males	23	72	25	30	14	164	3.3659	1.1828
Females	13	49	8	35	4	109	3.294	1.149
Total	36	121	33	65	18	273		

$X^2 = 11.22 > 9.49 = X^2_{(.05;\, df = 4)}$

Decision: Reject H_0

There is a relationship between gender and response to B1 (iv).

Table 4.3.1b Relationship between gender and response to item BI (v)

H_0: There are no gender differences in responses to B1 (v)

H_1: There are gender differences in responses to B1 (v)

GENDER	RESPONSES						Mean Score	S.D
	SA	A	U	D	SD	Total		
Males	33	75	26	25	5	164	3.6463	1.061
Females	19	66	4	15	4	108	3.75	1.0242
Total	52	141	30	40	9	273		

$X^2 = 12.07 > 9.49 = X^2_{(.05;\ df = 4)}$

Decision: Reject H_0

There is a relationship between gender and response to B1 (v)

Table 4.3.2a Relationship between gender and response to item B2 (ii)

H_0: There is no relationship between gender and response to B2 (ii)

H_1: There is a relationship between gender and response to B2 (ii)

GENDER	RESPONSES						Mean Score	S.D
	SA	A	U	D	SD	Total		
Males	41	54	13	24	32	164	3.293	1.478
Females	30	44	6	7	23	110	3.464	1.482
Total	71	98	19	31	55	274		

$X^2 = 5.68 < 9.49 = X^2_{(.05;\ df = 4)}$

Decision: Retain H_0

There is no relationship between gender and response to B2 (ii)

Table 4.3.2b Relationship between gender and response to item B2 (v) (b)

H_0: There are no gender difference in responses to B2 (v) (b)

H_1: There are gender differences in responses to B2 (v) (b)

GENDER	RESPONSES						Mean Score	S.D
	SA	A	U	D	SD	Total		
Males	16	62	22	30	36	166	2.952	1.348
Females	23	37	12	23	13	108	3.315	1.344
Total	39	99	34	53	49	274		

$X^2 = 10.42 > 9.49 = X^2_{(.05;\ df = 4)}$

Decision: Reject H_0

There are gender differences in responses to B2 (v) (b)

Table 4.3.3a Relationship between gender and response to item B3 (iii)

H_0: There are no gender differences in responses to B3 (iii)

H_1: There are gender differences in responses to B3 (iii)

GENDER	RESPONSES						Mean Score	S.D
	SA	A	U	D	SD	Total		
Males	102	55	2	7	2	168	4.4762	0.8186
Females	52	43	7	7	1	110	4.2545	0.903
Total	154	98	9	14	3	278		

$X^2 = 9.11 < 9.49 = X^2_{(.05;\ df = 4)}$

Decision: Retain H_0

There are no gender differences in responses to B3 (iii)

Table 4.3.3b Relationship between gender and response to item B3 (v)

H_0: There are no gender differences in responses to B3 (v)

H_1: There are gender differences in responses to B2 (v)

GENDER	RESPONSES						Mean Score	S.D
	SA	A	U	D	SD	Total		
Males	6	15	10	45	90	166	1.8072	1.1223
Females	7	5	2	46	50	110	1.845	1.102
Total	13	20	12	91	140	276		

$X^2 = 10.94 > 9.49 = X^2_{(.05;\ df = 4)}$

Decision: Reject H_0

There are gender differences in responses to B3 (v)

Table 4.3.4a Relationship between Mathematics specialisation and response to item B1 (iii)

H_0: Mathematics specialisation has no influence on responses to B1 (iii)

H_1: Mathematics specialisation has an influence on responses to B1 (iii)

MAIN SUBJECT	RESPONSES						Mean Score	S.D
	SA	A	U	D	SD	Total		
Maths	6	9	1	6	4	26	2.731	1.458
Non-Maths	76	114	7	42	19	249	2.1807	1.158
Total	82	123	8	48	14	275		

$X^2 = 7.68 < 9.49 = X^2_{(.05;\ df = 4)}$

Decision: Retain H_0

Mathematics specialisation has no influence on responses to B1 (iii)

Table 4.3.4b Relationship between Mathematics specialisation and response to item B1 (iv)

H_0: Mathematics specialisation has no influence on responses to B1 (iv)

H_1: Mathematics specialisation has an influence on responses to B1 (iv)

MAIN SUBJECT	RESPONSES						Mean Score	S.D
	SA	A	U	D	SD	Total		
Maths	6	8	6	6	0	26	3.577	0.987
Non-Maths	30	113	27	59	18	247	3.6992	1.053
Total	36	121	33	65	18	273		

$X^2 = 8.09 < 9.49 = X^2_{(.05;\ df = 4)}$

Decision: Retain H_0

Mathematics specialisation has no influence on responses to B1 (iv)

Table 4.3.4c Relationship between Mathematics specialisation and response to item B2 (i) (e)

H_0**:** Mathematics specialisation has no influence on responses to B2 (i) (e)

H_1**:** Mathematics specialisation has an influence on responses to B2 (i) (e)

MAIN SUBJECT	RESPONSES						Mean Score	S.D
	SA	A	U	D	SD	Total		
Maths	0	1	3	13	8	25	1.88	0.781
Non-Maths	8	68	33	101	35	245	2.6449	1.127
Total	8	69	36	114	43	270		

$X^2 = 10.96 > 9.49 = X^2_{(.05;\ df = 4)}$

Decision: Reject H_0

Mathematics specialisation has an influence on responses to B2 (i) (e)

Table 4.3.4d Relationship between Mathematics specialisation and response to item B5 (iv)

H_0: Mathematics specialisation has no influence on responses to B1 (iv)

H_1: Mathematics specialisation has an influence on responses to B1 (iv)

MAIN SUBJECT	RESPONSES						Mean Score	S.D
	SA	A	U	D	SD	Total		
Maths	6	12	1	7	0	26	4.654	1.129
Non-Maths	46	157	18	24	6	251	3.8486	0.913
Total	52	169	19	31	6	277		

$X^2 = 8.67 < 9.49 = X^2_{(.05;\ df = 4)}$

Decision: Retain H_0

Mathematics specialisation has no influence on responses to B5 (iv)

Table 4.3.5a Relationship between years of teaching experience and response to item B2 (ii)

H_0: There is no relationship between teaching experience and response to B2 (ii)

H_1: There is a relationship between teaching experience and response to B2 (ii)

TEACHING EXPERIENCE (Yrs)	RESPONSES						Mean Score	S.D
	SA	A	U	D	SD	Total		
0	45	48	10	12	23	138	3.58	1.444
1 - 3	19	41	6	11	24	101	3.198	1.483
4 +	4	8	2	7	6	27	2.889	1.45
Total	68	97	18	30	53	266		

$X^2 = 14.31 < 15.51 = X^2_{(.05;\ df = 8)}$

Decision: retain H_0

There is no relationship between teaching experience and response to B2 (ii)

Table 4.3.5b Relationship between years of teaching experience and response in item B3 (iv)

H_0: There is no relationship between teaching experience and response to B3 (iv)

H_1: There is a relationship between teaching experience and response to B3 (iv)

TEACHING EXPERIENCE (Yrs)	RESPONSES						Mean Score	S.D
	SA	A	U	D	SD	Total		
0	38	58	11	19	11	137	2.321	1.242
1 - 3	28	40	5	20	10	103	2.456	1.334
4 +	6	10	1	3	7	27	2.815	1.57
Total	72	108	17	42	28	267		

$X^2 = 10.33 < 15.51 = X^2_{(.05;\, df = 8)}$

Decision: Retain H_0

There is no relationship between teaching experience and response to B3 (iv)

Table 4.3.5c Relationship between years of teaching experience and response to item B5 (iv)

H_0: There is no relationship between teaching experience and response to B5 (iv)

H_1: There is a relationship between teaching experience and response to B5 (iv)

TEACHING EXPERIENCE (Yrs)	RESPONSES						Mean Score	S.D
	SA	A	U	D	SD	Total		
0	23	89	7	15	3	137	3.8321	0.912
1 - 3	22	60	7	14	1	104	3.8462	0.943
4 +	5	14	5	2	1	27	3.741	0.984
Total	50	163	19	31	5	268		

$X^2 = 9.06 < 15.51 = X^2_{(.05;\, df = 8)}$

Decision: Retain H_0

There is no relationship between teaching experience and response to B3 (iv)

Table 4.3.6a Relationship between age of the student and response to item B5 (i)

H_0: There is no relationship between age of the student and response to B5 (i)

H_1: There is a relationship between age of the student and response to B5 (i)

AGE (Yrs)	RESPONSES						Mean Score	S.D
	SA	A	U	D	SD	Total		
20 - 22	23	34	9	8	7	81	3.716	1.227
23 - 25	30	65	15	8	6	124	3.8468	1.02
26 +	16	28	17	10	1	72	0.667	1.021
Total	69	127	41	26	14	277		

$X^2 = 14.66 < 15.51 = X^2_{(.05;\ df = 8)}$

Decision: Retain H_0

There is no relationship between age of the student and response to B5 (i)

Table 4.3.6b Relationship between age of the student and response to item B5 (iii)

H_0: There is no significant differences in responses by age for B5 (iii)

H_1: There are significant differences in responses by age for B5 (iii)

AGE (Yrs)	RESPONSES						Mean Score	S.D
	SA	A	U	D	SD	Total		
20 - 22	16	47	14	4	0	81	3.9259	0.755
23 - 25	40	57	23	4	1	125	4.048	0.841
26 +	22	34	11	2	3	72	3.972	0.978
Total	78	138	48	10	4	278		

$X^2 = 10.58 < 15.51 = X^2_{(.05;\ df = 8)}$

Decision: Retain H_0

There are no significant differences in responses by age for B5 (iii)

Table 4.3.6c Relationship between age and response to item B5 (iv)

H_0: There are no significant differences in responses by age for B5 (iv)

H_1: There are significant differences in responses by age for B5 (iv)

AGE (Yrs)	RESPONSES						Mean Score	S.D
	SA	A	U	D	SD	Total		
20 - 22	7	64	1	9	0	81	3.8519	0.727
23 - 25	32	64	9	14	5	124	3.8387	1.062
26 +	13	41	9	8	1	72	3.792	0.918
Total	52	169	19	31	6	277		

$X^2 = 25.06 > 15.51 = X^2_{(.05;\ df = 8)}$

Decision: Reject H_0

There are significant differences in responses by age for B5 (iv)

ABOUT THE AUTHOR

Mr. Barnabas Muyengwa is a lecturer and National Programme Leader for the Bachelor of Education in Curriculum Studies and the Post Graduate Diploma in Education (PGDE) in the Faculty of Arts and Education in the Department of Teacher Development at the Zimbabwe Open University (ZOU). He has published in international peer reviewed research journals. He has presented research papers at international and local conferences. Before joining ZOU he was a principal lecturer at Seke Teachers' College in the Mathematics Department. He can be contacted by business address: Zimbabwe Open University P.O.Box MP1119 Mount Pleasant Harare, Zimbabwe or by mobile phone: +263 772 238 397 or by e-mail: muyengwabb@gmail.com